TROUT

THE GAME & FISH MASTERY LIBRARY

TROUT

By S. G. B. Tennant, Jr.
Photography by Arie deZanger

WILLOW CREEK PRESS

Minocqua, Wisconsin

Food photographs © Arie deZanger
Food stylist: Wilma deZanger

Fly fishing and underwater trout
photographs © by Denver Bryan:
Pages 7, 8, 13, 14, 43, 71

Published by Willow Creek Press
P.O. Box 147
Minocqua, Wisconsin 54548

For information on other Willow Creek titles, call 1-800-850-9453

Library of Congress Cataloging-in-Publication Data

Tennant, S.G.B.
    Trout / by S.G.B. Tennant, Jr. ; photography by Arie deZanger.
      p. cm. -- (The game & fish mastery library)
    ISBN 1-57223-276-5
    1. Cookery (Trout) I. Title. II. Series.

   TX748.T74 T46 2000
   641.6'92--dc21   99-086913

Printed in Canada

TABLE OF CONTENTS

ACKNOWLEDGMENTS

There are no more devoted conservationists than you will find in the wild trout movement. TROUT UNLIMITED is leading the way with web sites and a full scale national organization. To find out what you can do, write:

TROUT UNLIMITED
1500 Wilson Boulevard, Suite 310
Arlington, VA 22209 - 2404
(703) 522-0200
To join or renew: 800- 834-2419-2419
http://www.tu.org.

It doesn't stop there. The web is alive with a contant rising hatch of offerings from Sierra Trout (a conservation group spearheaded by Greg Imarti), to trade groups listing all the rainbow trout hatcheries with products for sale in western North Carolina.

Trout cookery is enthusiastically alive as well, and the production of this book was supported by a host of suppliers and creative hatcheries. I visited with Jon and Resa Wallach who supplied many of the trout in these pictures. They are one of the main sources for the novel *Troutlings*.

Resa and Jon Wallach
Eden Brook Hatchery
1327 Cold Springs Road,
Forestburgh NY 12777
914 796 1749

Some of the best smoked trout to be found was provided by:
Tom Marshal, of
Homarus, Inc.
76 Kisco Avenue,
Mt Kisco NY 10549-149
914-666-8992

The studio work was brightened up with props from :
Patio Classic Grills/Porcelain Metals, Inc. 1- 800 585 47445, and the essential and glamorous Cuisinart 1-800 726 0190.

Marty Keane, of Classic Rods & Tackles, Inc. was a rock on sorting out the history of my old bamboo rods, and studio assistant Ryan Silbaugh in Sugar Loaf, New York made the photos work.

S.G.B.T.Jr.

INTRODUCTION

Many years ago a friend invited me to fish a hidden trout stream that the Brink's family had cultivated outside Cody, Wyoming. It was a brilliant, lively stream, with cold fresh water cascading down and around a steep mountainside, through transparent pools with sanding bottoms, and ending with a fish gate, or weir, across the water.

And every bend in that stream was bubbling with small brook trout. And every cast into that beauty was retrieved in splendid tranquility. It was an extraordinary experience. After a few hours, I realized the secret to my success, and the hidden charm of the place. All the really dangerous tree limbs had been previously sawed away.

Every rising fish was a possibility, and there wasn't much time spent disentangling your leader from the flora. The care paid by the owners to every detail, even to the placement of an occasional wading stone to cross the stream, showed the immense dedication of trout fishermen who loved their sport.

Years later, as I waded through the literature of trout fishing, I found the same intensity had been the hallmark of every great writer on the subject. Vince Marinaro, a tax lawyer from Philadelphia, would agonize at length over the choice between silk thread versus horsehair for tying his magnificent ant imitations.

Detail was everything with Marinaro, as it is with the thousands of devoted trout fishermen who consider their river time to be their best. And this book has been a lot like that. I had to choose from the thousands of trout recipes that I have tried at streamside or in the kitchen, and tried to narrow the list to the exceptional, and the absolutely necessary, while still having a little fun.

With cookbooks, just as with dining itself, the first impression is half the battle. So I must offer a loud salute to Wilma and Arie deZanger who have artfully and meticulously illustrated my recipes in their inimitable style, always preserving the essence of the original idea, and adding something in the bargain.

Fifteen years ago Arie and I were on a 'film' shoot on location, and at the end of the day, we actually had to catch fish for dinner. He asked me how I meant to cook it, and I said, "Let's have a flip through Julia Child."

And that was the way it was for me for as many years as I've been swinging a spatula. Originally, I would turn to the works of Escoffier, or Pellaprat or Prosper Montagne. Then later came James Beard and Michael Field. But nobody put the sheep in the pen quite like Julia Child.

As I have said elsewhere, it is her hard work, her largely self-taught experience and her simple refusal to take herself too seriously that makes her such a reliable mentor. My original copies of *Mastering the Art of French Cooking* and *In Julia's Kitchen* are worn through and rebound in sturdy buckram bindings to stand the strain of constant kitchen usage.

And with that usage has come a respect for some of the things she did beyond the cookbooks. The most important of these was to raise the public consciousness about the fun of food, and the honorable pleasure to be gained by doing something for yourself and your friends, like cooking.

Every fish and game challenge I've had in the kitchens of the world began with the same question: how did the masters handle this one? And the second question was always: what can we do to make it more fun? That is my foundation in fish and game cooking, but I know it would be less well informed but for the work of Julia Child. And so with a heartfelt "thank you" and a modest trepidation, please allow me to dedicate these efforts to Julia Child, America's Master Gastronome.

It's been great fun putting this series together and I hope that all dry fly-fishermen and dab hands in the kitchen will use the grand and ready supply of hatchery trout in the markets, together with their own precious supply of wild fish, to enjoy what so many for so long have considered the joys of the most exquisite fish.

Good Cooking!

— S.G.B. Tennant, Jr.,

Helena, Texas

A Trout in the Kitchen

When you get down to cases in the kitchen, or for that matter at fireside, there are only two kinds of trout: small and large.

There is not one sauce for brook trout and one sauce for brown trout. The canon of known "trout" recipes, the *amandine*, the *en papillote*, and the *meunière* apply with equal charm to the Dolly Varden or the grayling, neither of which are actually of the trout species in the strict taxonomic sense, but rather char.

Trout in the kitchen are distinguished from all other fish by their unique culinary qualities — their delicate flavor, texture and leanness. The objective of the trout cook, using ritual and mystery in equal parts, is to maximize this flavor and preserve this delicate texture. After 200 years of enlightened trout cookery, those of us who stand around in the kitchen a lot have isolated a short list of dishes favored by serious diners. In most cases the choice is dictated by the size of the trout, not his species.

A small trout poached in fresh milk and a few handfuls of the bright sorrel which once were so common in the kitchen gardens of Britain and Ireland work for the brown trout native to Britain. But it also works for the American rainbow, and the arctic char.

The late M.F.K. Fisher, always a discerning cook and student of good food, kept only one picture in her kitchen. In the place she called "Last House" she hung a painting of "trout meunière," its crisp butter coating over delicate trout flesh beckoning and uncompromising. That single bit of artistry described her kitchen and her cooking, while the other wall was given out to a window on the mountains.

The chef's art in the kitchen, however, lies in stretching these traditional recipes, and in blending ingredients. The brook trout served in amandine fashion with its filet sautéed in butter and oil and shrouded in blanched almonds, set against a delicate whiff of lemon juice and sherry to heighten the bouquet, branches into kitchen alchemy.

The trail of small trout cookery spirals upward from there, including delicate mousses and whole fish wrapped in exotic blankets. Each of these require trout well under two pounds, which have fed exclusively on insects when taken from the wild, and are uniform and boned when produced from the trout farm.

Smallness in trout is a virtue. In the Chinese kitchen, the miniature fish were often steamed in elaborate bamboo and wood racks that stacked efficiently over a steaming wok. The whole fish was used, and the shared essence of the fish juices produced by the steaming lent flavor and context back to the puddled rice.

In old Soo-Chow, once an ancient provincial Chinese capital but today only a suburb of Shanghai, the thousand lakes were famous for their small fish, and small and beautiful maidens. In those country kitchens they fried whole, small trout, puffed up in billows of egg to ensure an even cooking that protects the flesh against drying. The short cooking times and high heat so necessary here are only possible when one uses the diminutive form of fish.

The very small troutlings netted out of the hatchery and deep fried in seconds are a modern miracle. The cooking technique is the same as the Chinese used, but the scale is different because we have been able to use fish no bigger than a pub dart, and only five months old. When fried up in cracker crumbs without a batter you have the very essence of small trout cooking, fast and tasty.

I have read a few of the haughty condescensions directed at the table quality of farm-raised trout and I must object. Those comments are dated, and cannot be accepted as a rule today without qualification. Water quality, food supply and post-harvest handling are the three most important considerations for any table fish, regardless of the source. Numerous recent advances suggest that good farm trout can be the equal of any wild caught fish.

Over the history of the great kitchens, clever chefs have continually experimented with trout presentations, but the essentials have remained constant. The trout was always cooked under wraps, quickly and without loss of succulence or flavor.

In Monte Carlo at the old Hotel Paris they wrapped the fish in lettuce leaves to protect its succulence. In the Northern Italian cuisines they used the finest cured prosciutto to coddle the flavor from the little trout brought down from the mountains. And even the celebrated Jacques Pepin still recommends the old Pellaprat *en papillote* technique to preserve moisture and subtly blend the seasonings with the fish. Snip open the hot paper bag as it comes to the table, and whiff the appetizing prelude to your meal.

Escoffier had his own list of favorites, and offered trout accompanied by at least nine different mousse recipes, one for every occasion. He had mousse of crayfish, one of strawberry, a tomato, and even grilled red peppers. Our choice here, "Turbans of Trout" were so popular in formal *belle époque* cuisine that even jaded palettes were known to push forward in the buffet. The bright butter sauce added here is a tribute to Wilma and Arie deZanger who are enthusiastic and sophisticated "Dutch foodies."

At one time between the wars, perhaps seventy years

ago, the small country kitchens of Provence regularly served trout with a red wine sauce. It was likewise so in Britain and America, but the practice is almost completely reversed these days. It is important to recall the charm of the red wine sauces as used here in the "Trout Macon."

By convention in those days, small trout were usually served with head on, and more importantly, bones in. As American popular tastes and sensibilities have come recently to accept fish, and to deal with the challenges of the occasional fish bone, there has been in our country a very healthy if limited acceptance of the whole fish as food.

The advantages to the diner are found in the more natural appearance, and in an added richness in the sauce. But tastes weren't always this way, of course.

Everybody talks about "blue trout," but they are rarely eaten in America. "Truite Bleu," in the bible of gastronomy, is fish poached within ten minutes of leaving the stream or holding pool, cleaned through the gills, and served with a dab of mayonnaise on a linen napkin. It is the very apotheosis of fresh fish.

The blue skin color of the cooked fish demonstrates its freshness and is a reaction of the surface film on the living fish to the heat of cooking. Like most other shibboleths, the search for the blue color became an objective in itself requiring more and more vinegar in the poaching liquid and more and more artful devices to induce the fish to curl sharply, nose to tail when presented to the diner.

But among anglers there are also connoisseurs. The wild mountains of Montana from Varney Bridge to Three Forks will forever echo with the voice of Jack Love from Sheridan, his Stetson crammed down on his head, standing in back of his river boat and fighting a rainbow on the Madison River. On the far shore his children dutifully stoked the campfire under a steaming kettle.

When the net slipped over the fish Jack bellowed out, "Power on!" and his boatman hewed into the oars, rowing mightily across the current to reach the fire in record time.

Another mountain favorite was smoking or grilling when you had a trout of respectable size. Grilled trout, whether done on a griddle, plank or with a wire basket over a dull fire, is always my choice for alfresco cooking because of the simplicity of it all, with only a squeeze of lemon at hand. In a backyard setting, the kited and grilled fish benefit from a fresh fruit contrast like a very hip "Barbados Fruit Splash" developed in honor of distant island friends.

Smoked trout are a tradition on western lakes and waters where old smokehouses still stand beside their much loved lakes. Slow smoking can cure even a two-pound fish, but in spite of their holding quality, smoked fish are best eaten right away.

There are many ways to "stuff" a fish with a forcemeat, or ground fish and flavors, and they all have long histories. Trout Chambord traces its character back to an eponymous castle in France that kept a stable of 1200 hunters and jumpers, a monumental collection of old weapons, and a cooking staff that looked like a cavalry brigade.

Any forcemeat will do, but small shrimp jumped into recognition by a blend of peppers round out the flavor cycle and provide a contrast. It is worth noting that farm trout, wholly boned, absorb flavors better from the exposed inner flesh than do fish dressed in the conventional manner with the bones still in.

Another *en casserole* presentation of trout comes from a bit of good luck we had in finding an English pub with a trout lunch. I had coyly suggested to our hostess Barbara Castle, the recently created Barroness of Blackburn, that I, a mere commoner and a foreigner to boot, was going down to have some fishing on the River Test that day. My wife and I promised to bring back a trout or two for dinner.

That bit of bravado invoked all the deities who dish out hubris, and put the "kebash" on the enterprise from the outset. Barbara's dog Teddy, with a fine disregard for the etiquette of the river, lost interest in watching me fish and dove into the Test, determined to catch the trout himself. All onlookers were horrified, and we left in shame.

Rather than ask to kill a fish on this river, we drove an extra hour out of the way on the route home scouting up a restaurant with a fishy bill of fare.

We found a country pub in the village of Thame, talked our way into the kitchen and started recalling the half remembered ingredients for Trout Montbarry, sort of a grilled trout with omelette combination. Out of that very happy exchange came "A Trout for the Barroness Blackburn." As we sat in the bar with smoke-colored wood panels and a few cricket trophies over the mantle won by the Gray's Lane Irregulars, we vowed that this dish had a great future, and I hope you agree.

But all trout are not small and one pan size cannot accomodate all the mysteries of trout. Larger fish offer magnificent taste opportunities in addition to the sporting awe they generate. These large fish, which dine upon other fish, give the cook great scope for the seasonings and sauces that make up, for instance, a hot fish soup.

For the *matelote* or fish stew, the French hew out great chunks of large trout filets, medallions of meat capable of supporting the big flavors of garlic, onion and thyme. This dish requires the utmost attention to the balance of flavors in the sauce, and a big loaf of bread, such as the Scottish Rant Bread, to balance the textures and magnify the experience.

Big American trout like the steelhead, have a higher fat content and a very distinctive flavor. It follows that wherever he now lies in the taxonomy sweepstakes, the steelhead is a big, red, trout-like fish, and he can and should carry a big sauce. The watercress and potato sauce used here in "Red Trout/Green Sauce" is an old standby developed by A.J. McClane, and doctored around over the years.

In certain posh European restaurants one occasionally encounters a reference to "Salmon Trout," but these are only the same large brown trout, sometimes sea run and with a slightly pink flesh that are always cooked in trout fashion.

On the other hand, if it looks like a trout and it cooks like a trout, it will taste like a trout. And so without even a shiver of irony I have included here the very popular spotted seatrout, which isn't a trout at all, except to the thousands of fishermen who catch and eat them every day.

This seatrout (one word) is actually classified as a "drum" but has all the important trout credentials. I have smoked, poached and moussed this first cousin to the squeateague and the spotted weakfish, and he is as fine as any of the large trout. The flesh is white, firm and mild flavored, and the fatty or oil content is comparable or less than that of the steelhead. In the liberated kitchen, we will not be captives of taxonomy.

But down in Swansea, on the South Coast of Wales, you will find some of the finest sea trout (two words) fishing. These are anadromous brown trout who have spent some time in the ocean and come home to be caught in the coastal river and baked in large breaded filets in the oven.

Traditionally, the Welsh ate seaweed (*popyrous anethyon*) as a side dish with this baked fish. Mixed with cereal it brought to the table a slightly salty taste of the sea with a hint of oysters. It was harvested as a found vegetable, clinging to rocks in the littoral zone, dried, pounded and then reconstituted. They called it "laverbread" and it was free from the sea, proof of the fact that the Gods were smiling on the Welsh valleys. With the advent of sliced bread, the old ways have sadly dropped from sight.

It was a foreign chef, George Soyer, *gros bonnet* and imperium of the Reform Club in London in the 19th century, who tried to rekindle an interest in laver and laverbread. But today, only the most traditional of kitchens in Wales still savors the slight oyster-sea flavor that the laver brings to a meal.

Trout will also rise to the challenge of garlic and wine or any other delicate presentation. And whether they be from hatchery or sparkling stream, the chef's greatest joy, always, is to have a trout in the kitchen.

TROUT EN PAPILLOTE NICOISE

Each paper tent serves as an individual steam chamber infusing the fish with the Provençal flavors
of onion, olive and garlic. When the tent is sliced open at table, an aromatic puff welcomes each guest.

2 brook trout — whole, fins removed
3 Tablespoons olive oil
1 cup sliced mushrooms
2 Tablespoons sliced onions
1 Tablespoon garlic, minced

1 cup white wine
2 Tablespoons sliced olives
1 teaspoon dried oregano
1 teaspoon tomato paste
salt and pepper

Lightly coat the fish in garlic, olive oil, salt and pepper and set aside.

In a saucepan over moderate heat, soften the 3 Tablespoons of olive oil and sauté the mushrooms, onion and garlic for 10 minutes without browning. Add the wine, olives, oregano and, over medium high heat, reduce the wine to a syrupy essence, barely enough sauce to cover the two fish. Set aside.

Prepare the parchment papillotes as large heart shaped pieces. (*For an illustrated description of this procedure, see pages 82-83 under Culinary Procedures.*) One half of the heart should be large enough to accommodate at least 2 inches of free space around the perimeter of the fish. Place an equal amount of the sauce down the center of one half of the heart. Cover the sauce with the fish, and spoon some sauce inside the cavity of the fish. Seal the filets by folding up the edges as demonstrated on page 83. After sealing, turn the sealed papillote over so that the folded edges are down. Send the papillotes to the oven immediately.

In a preheated oven of 400°F bake the papillotes on a lower shelf on a clean baking sheet for 5 minutes. Fish thicker than ¾ inch may take a minute longer. The paper will brown and puff up from the sealed steam. Remove from the oven and allow the papillotes to rest for 2 minutes before serving.

Serve each fish in its papillote on an individual plate, with garnish. Allow each guest to open the envelope with a sharp bladed knife, releasing the bouquet, and serving themselves from the paper.

Water Angels of Soo-Chow

In medieval China, small trout were kept in holding traps along the streams and fried up in billows
of frothy egg white batter, with just a touch of starch to bind the egg to the whole fish, subtly flavored with the brown sugar and wine.

2 rainbow trout—all fins removed, cleaned & wiped dry
2 Tablespoons lemon juice
3 Tablespoons onion pulp
1 garlic clove, crushed and minced
3 egg whites
¼ cup white wine (or Chinese Saki)

¼ teaspoon salt
¼ teaspoon brown sugar
½ teaspoon corn starch
1 Tablespoon dried ginger, freshly ground
vegetable oil for frying

Wash and dry the fish thoroughly inside and out with paper towels. Brush the fish inside with a mixture of the lemon juice, onion pulp and garlic. Set aside.

Whisk the egg whites to stiff peaks. Combine the wine, salt, sugar and starch and add this to the egg whites. Continue whisking until thoroughly combined.

Preheat a wok or deep kettle with 3 inches of oil to 400°F. Dry the trout again with paper towels and lightly season with salt and pepper. Roll the trout lightly in the egg white mixture, leaving the head and tail clean and free of the egg, and fry until golden brown. Serve with a sprinkle of ground ginger over the fish.

Trout Macon Lyonnaise

*In small country restaurants in France they have always used red wine sauces for whole trout. When the sauce is boiled up
from the cooking wine and reduced with a bit of meat glaze, the flavors run together in the brown rich tones of onions and mushrooms.*

4 whole dressed trout — ½ pound each
2 cups red wine
¼ teaspoon dried thyme
2 Tablespoons olive oil
1 clove garlic, diced
4 Tablespoons butter
½ cup beef bouillon
½ teaspoon salt

¼ teaspoon sugar
2 cups of small mushroom caps, whole (or sliced canterelles)
1 teaspoon meat demi-glaze
1 Tablespoon arrowroot
2 cups onions, sliced thin
salt and pepper
parsley to garnish

Lightly salt and pepper the trout inside and out and place in a baking pan large enough for all. Add the wine, a pinch of thyme, and the minced garlic. Then bake, basting but not turning, in a preheated 350°F oven for 12-15 minutes, or until the trout flakes at the tip of a knife. Remove from the oven and arrange the trout side by side on a serving platter, and keep warm. Reserve the wine.

In a sauté pan over low heat, soften 3 Tablespoons of butter, add the sliced onions, and sauté for 5 minutes until the onions begin to color slightly. Add enough bouillon to cover the onions. Add the salt and sugar and

continue to simmer until the liquid has evaporated and the onions are glazed. Remove the onions with a slotted spoon to one end of the large serving platter with the fish, and keep warm.

In the same pan sauté the mushrooms in 2 Tablespoons of olive oil until they are tender but not thoroughly cooked, approximately 10 minutes. To the same saucepan add the wine drained from the trout and reduce it slightly over high heat. With a slotted spoon remove the mushrooms to one end of the serving platter.

To the saucepan add the demi-glaze. Blend the arrowroot with the remaining 1 Tablespoon butter and

TROUT MACON LYONNAISE (CONTINUED)

add this to the saucepan. Mix well. Boil this, then remove from the heat, then boil again, stirring frequently. Remove from the heat and adjust seasoning.

Pour all the sauce over the trout, and serve with the glazed onions at one end of the platter and the mushrooms at the other. Garnish with parsley.

Smoked Trout Soup

Supplies of precious smoked trout quickly change the character of a good stock and together they produce the ambrosia of smoked soup. This robust soup will accommodate any real bread, and scones with a hint of cheese make it a meal.

1½ cups smoked trout — skinned and boned (9 ounces)
1 cup onions, sliced
1 cup celery tips, sliced
1 cup shiitake mushrooms, sliced
2 Tablespoons olive oil
2 Tablespoons butter
1 Tablespoon bouquet garni, in a sachet bag or infuser

4 cups fish fumet (see page 73 for recipe) or chicken stock, fat removed
salt and pepper
4 Tablespoons heavy cream
2 Tablespoons fresh parsley, chopped
2 Tablespoons dry sherry

Prepare the trout by picking the meat out of the fish, discarding all bones and skin.

In a large Dutch oven on top of the stove, sauté the onions and celery in the butter over medium heat until they become translucent, but not browned. Add the mushrooms and continue the sauté until they soften. Add the stock, the sachet or infuser of bouquet garni, and bring to boil. Reduce the heat and simmer for 30 minutes.

Add the smoked trout meat and continue the simmer for 15 minutes. Remove the bouquet garni and discard. Purée the soup in a food processor and return the soup to the Dutch oven. Adjust the seasonings with salt and pepper, add the cream and simmer gently until the soup thickens slightly.

Serve in individual bowls with a spoon of sherry and a garnish of parsley floating on each serving, along with a basket of Cheddar Scones *(see page 78)*.

Rainbow Wrap

In the north of Italy the finest prosciutto, salt cured and pressed, is a wrap for many dishes.
Around fresh trout, the delicate ham wrapping cooks along with the fish and contributes a subtle seasoning.

4 rainbow trout — cleaned, boned, heads on. All dorsal,
    pectoral and adipose fins should be removed
8-12 slices prosciutto, cured but uncooked, sliced thin
1 Tablespoon olive oil
1 teaspoon dried thyme

4 Tablespoons butter
salt and fresh ground pepper
2 Tablespoons sherry
2 parsley stalks

Lightly season each fish with salt and pepper, inside and out. Place a pinch (¼ teaspoon) of dried thyme inside each cavity and fold closed. Lightly rub scant olive oil over the outside of each trout, including head and tail.

    Wrap each fish in 2 or 3 sheets of prosciutto and place all fish in a large broiler pan. Divide the butter into small slivers and apply it to the tops of the prosciutto, equally apportioned among the fish. Add the sherry to the pan. Broil the fish in a preheated broiler (375°F) for approximately 12 minutes, basting until the prosciutto begins to color. Remove when the fish is cooked.

    Serve immediately with the pan juices spooned over each fish and parsley for garnish.

TURBANS OF TROUT WITH CILANTRO MOUSSE

Fashion for its own sake inspired the turbans of the belle époque. With the addition
of a bright mustard sauce, the trout and mousse are more than just another pretty mouthful.

4 trout filets — skinned, bones removed
1 Tablespoon sherry
2 egg yolks, beaten slightly
¼ teaspoon cayenne pepper
½ teaspoon each of salt and pepper
4 Tablespoons heavy cream
2 egg whites, beaten to soft peaks
4 cups cilantro with some stems, chopped

1 cup parsley, chopped
2 Tablespoons fresh chives, minced
1 leaf of basil, torn into small bits
½ clove garlic, pressed
olive oil for lining the timbales
4 individual molds or timbales, 3 inches wide by 2 inches tall,
   6 ounce capacity

Dry the filets, then salt and pepper them lightly on both sides and refrigerate pending final assembly. Refrigerate the processor bowl and blade. (*See pages 86-87 for an illustrated description of forming the Turbans of Trout.*)

Oil the timbales, and fold 1 filet into each, with the white side of the fish to the outside, pressing the fish against the sides of the timbale. This will leave a small opening at the 'bottom' of the timbale. Trim away any overhanging fish so that the turban will sit evenly on the serving platter after cooking. Refrigerate the timbales until needed.

Parboil the cilantro and parsley in boiling water for 2 minutes. Remove, rinse in cold water, drain, pat dry, wrap in paper towels, and refrigerate. In a processor bowl combine the cilantro, parsley, chives, basil leaf, and garlic purée, and process for 10 seconds.

In a small bowl combine the eggs, sherry, cayenne, salt and pepper and beat slightly. Add the egg mixture to the cilantro mixture, and process for 10 seconds. In a bowl, whisk the egg whites until they hold slight peaks. Add this mixture to the processor bowl, and blend for 5 seconds.

In a bowl, beat the cream with a whisk until it holds slight peaks. Add this mixture to the processor bowl and blend for 10 seconds until thoroughly combined. Spoon the mousse into each timbale, and smooth flat at the top.

Place all 4 timbales in an open roasting pan. Add enough boiling water to reach ⅓ of the way up the timbale, but not enough to float them. Cover loosely with aluminum foil and bake for at least 60 minutes in a pre-heated oven at 350°F. The mousse is cooked when it becomes firm and tends to draw away from the timbale.

Remove from the oven, invert the timbales on a rack, and allow to cool. Refrigerate for at least one hour. Decant the timbales onto a serving platter, and spoon a few tablespoons of DeZanger's Dutch Butter Sauce *(see page 75)* around the base of each.

THE TZAR'S LAST TROUT

Elia Tolstoy often told the bittersweet tale of a Russian nobleman whose last meal in St. Petersburg was a frenzied
but delicate combination of everything he loved, but was about to lose. The essence of the preparation was a heavy reduction
of stocks and spirits, and a very light cooking that allowed the shrimp and trout to maintain their integrity.

8 trout filets
12 raw shrimp
½ cup onion, minced finely
salt and pepper
2 bay leaves
1 stalk of celery
2 cups fish stock (or chicken stock)

2 cups white wine
2 Tablespoons Jamaican rum
¼ teaspoon of basil, thyme, and Chinese Sate seasoning
2 Tablespoons butter
1 cup parsley, chopped finely
2 Tablespoons dry sherry
1 Tablespoon butter

In a large saucepan combine the shrimp, onion, salt, bay leaves, celery and 2 cups of stock or water, and simmer over medium heat until the shrimp are done, about 10 minutes. Strain the resulting stock and reserve both the stock and the shrimp separately. Peel the shrimp, slice in half on the long axis, and reserve.

Over high heat in a saucepan, reduce the stock to about ½ cup. Remove from heat and add the wine, rum, basil, thyme and Chinese Sate seasoning to form a marinade. In a glass marinador, marinate the trout and sliced shrimp for 2 hours.

In a large sauté pan, poach the trout filets in the marinade with the addition of the sherry for 2-3 minutes. Remove the trout and keep warm. Raise the heat, and reduce the marinade to about 1½ cups and reserve. In a skillet toss the shrimp in butter to warm, then add the reduced marinade, stirring for one minute. Adjust the seasonings with salt and pepper. To serve, place a few shrimp slices over each filet and pour the marinade over the fish filets. Sprinkle with the chopped parsley.

Trout for the Baroness Blackburn

Fishing the River Test was meant to be an enobling experience, man against river, and so on. What we came away with was the memory of a cheerful country pub lunch, and a trout shirred in a mushroom and cheese omelette.

4 trout filets — boned, fins removed, skin on or off
salt and pepper
1 Tablespoon olive oil for greasing the pan
2 Tablespoons parsley, chopped
2 Tablespoons shallots, sliced paper thin
1 Tablespoons chives, chopped
1 teaspoon dried chervil
1 teaspoon dried tarragon leaves

4 Tablespoons fresh mushrooms, thinly sliced
2 Tablespoons butter, melted
2 Tablespoons olive oil
2 eggs, beaten
1 Tablespoon brandy
6 Tablespoons grated cheddar cheese (or swiss cheese)
6 Tablespoons stale bread crumbs
½ teaspoon paprika, to taste

Season the filets lightly with salt and pepper. In an oiled baking pan large enough to accommodate all filets without overlapping, scatter the parsley, shallots, chervil, tarragon and mushrooms.

Place the filets, skin side down without overlapping, over the herbs, and pour the olive oil and butter evenly over each filet.

In a preheated oven of 400°F cook the fish, uncovered, for 10 minutes.

While the filets are cooking, combine the cheese and bread crumbs in a small mixing bowl. In another mixing bowl beat the eggs and brandy until combined, and add salt and pepper.

Spoon the egg mixture over each filet. Then sprinkle the cheese and bread crumb mixture over each filet and add a dash of paprika for color. Return the baking pan to the oven and continue cooking, uncovered until the bread crumbs take on a golden color.

With a long spatula separate each serving. Garnish and send to the table with a half pint of bitter ale.

Grilled Brook Trout with Barbados Fruit Splash

Barbecue the trout just as they would in the Carribean, kited open and quickly cooked.
The sauce offers bright fruit flavors, with a hint of rum, that is straight from the beaches of old Barbados.

2 brook trout — dressed, boned (¾ pound each), skin on
olive oil
salt and pepper
2 cups pineapple chunks, skinned and cored
3 teaspoons green pepper sauce
1 cup fresh cilantro

2 Tablespoons fresh banana
¼ teaspoon each of salt and pepper
1 Tablespoon Mount Gay Rum
1 kiwi fruit, skinned
1 cup white grapefruit sections

Bring an electric or gas grill to the maximum heat, scrape or brush the grill surface, and then reduce the heat to low, and rub the grill surface with olive oil. Over a natural fire allow the grill itself to reach high heat and then shovel the coals away to one side or let them go gray. The objective is low, steady heat at the cooking site.

The trout should be "kited," or opened from the gills to the tail so that the fish will lie flat on the grill and cook evenly. Rub the trout all over with olive oil, then salt and pepper lightly, and place the fish skin side down on the grill for 2 minutes. Cover with a lid such as a roasting pan or aluminum foil sheet to contain the heat.

Using a long spatula, carefully loosen the skin from the grill, and lift and turn the fish. Cook the fish, flesh side down, for 2 minutes covered. Carefully turn the fish one time, baste with olive oil and continue cooking for 3 minutes further. Serve each fish, flesh up with a fruit salsa like the Barbados Splash.

The Barbados Splash is made in a processor bowl, combining the pineapple, pepper sauce, banana, salt and pepper and rum. Purée for 30 seconds, scraping down the sides to combine thoroughly. Spoon over the fish.

Skin each kiwi fruit and then slice each into thin full moon shapes. Arrange the kiwi slices and the grapefruit in alternate layers alongside the fish on the serving plate.

SALMON TROUT MATELOTE

The "salmon trout" is just a sea going brown trout with a year or two of offshore experience under his belt.
Thick filets, poached in the stock and wine, are brought back to the matelote after the velouté thickens
the broth. This legendary French fish soup was always eaten with a "big" bread, like the Scottish Rant bread.

4 cups, thick salmon trout filets, boned and skinned
(or lake trout)
1 cup shiitake mushrooms, sliced
1 cup onions, sliced thinly
2 cloves garlic, mashed and diced fine
1 cup fish stock (or clam juice)
1 bay leaf, crumbled
½ teaspoon thyme
2 Tablespoons olive oil
2 Tablespoons butter

2 teaspoons bouquet garni, in a bag or infuser
2 cups dry white wine
1 cup fish velouté sauce:
   2 Tablespoons butter
   2 Tablespoons flour
   ½ teaspoon cayenne pepper, ground
   1 cup of fish stock (or clam juice)
salt and pepper
1 cup pearl onions, skinned and parboiled for 5 minutes
1 cup parsley, chopped

In a large Dutch oven soften the sliced onions and garlic in the olive oil and butter for 5 mintues over low heat, but do not brown. Add the mushrooms, thyme and bay leaf and continue sautéeing for 5 minutes stirring constantly.

Add one cup of fish stock and 2 cups of wine and bring to a simmer for 5 minutes. Cut the fish into 1" x 2" chunks and add along with the bouquet garni. Cook for an additional 10 minutes. The fish is cooked when it flakes easily to the tip of a knife. Remove the fish and keep warm. Discard the bouquet garni, and thicken the sauce by adding the fish veloute sauce (recipe follows).

Fish velouté sauce: In a small saucepan combine the butter and oil and flour to form a white roux, and then slowly stir in the second cup of fish stock and the cayenne pepper until the mixture thickens. Add the velouté to the wine and mushroom sauce. Add the pearl onions and simmer for 10 minutes. Add the fish and allow it to warm through before serving in deep individual bowls with parsley and a loaf of the heroic Scottish Rant Bread (*see page 79*).

TRUITES A LA MEUNIÈRE

In the cottage she called "Last House," M.F.K. Fisher hung a single picture in her kitchen: a still-life
of Trout Meunière, butter and lemon fairly dripping from the canvas. No other trout presentation is more popular or accessible.

4 trout filets — skinned and boned
8 Tablespoons butter, to be clarified
4 Tablespoons flour for dusting
salt and pepper

2 Tablespoons olive oil
2 Tablespoons butter
2 Tablespoons lemon juice
5 Tablespoons parsley, chopped

Clarify 8 tablespoons of butter in a small saucepan over medium heat, skimming the foam off the surface. Allow the butter to cool. Spoon the clarified butter off the top of the mixture into a clean saucepan, and reserve for the sauce.

Wash and dry the trout filets. If they are more than 1 inch thick they should be flattened to ¾ inch in thickness. Season them with salt and pepper and dust them lightly with the flour. In a heavy skillet, soften 2 additional tablespoons of butter combined with the olive oil. When the foam subsides, add the filets and sauté over medium heat for about 3-5 minutes per side,

depending on the thickness of the filet, basting as you go to reach a good, brown color before turning. Turn only once, and cook until firm to the touch and golden brown. Remove the filets to a platter and keep warm.

In the saucepan over low heat, cook the clarified butter until it begins to brown, but not burn, and remove from the heat.

To serve, arrange the filets on a plate and sprinkle with the lemon juice and parsley. Pour the browned clarified butter over each filet. Serve immediately. Butter as a sauce prepared like this is called *beurre meunière*.

Spotted Seatrout Stuffed with Crab and Pepperflakes

*Along the Louisiana coast this seatrout and the crab swim together, and with a little help
from red pepper flakes, they rise to the dignity of any trout from any water.*

1 spotted seatrout, 2-3 pounds, scaled, gilled, and boned
1 cup cooked cornbread, crumbled
1 egg, broken
2 Tablespoons milk
2 Tablespoons parsley, chopped finely
½ teaspoon ground thyme
¼ teaspoon each of salt and pepper
2 Tablespoons olive oil
½ cup onion, chopped

1 cup mushrooms, sliced
1 cup cooked crabmeat
1 Tablespoon crushed red pepper flakes
2 Tablespoons lemon juice
2 teaspoons Worcestershire sauce
salt and pepper
butter for basting
½ cup dry sherry
1 cup water

Combine the egg and milk in a mixing bowl and stir briefly. Mix in the thyme, parsley, salt and pepper. Mix in the crumbled cornbread, the parsley and thyme.

In a sauté pan over low heat soften the onions, mushrooms and red pepper in the olive oil for 5-6 minutes but do not allow them to brown. Add the crabmeat, lemon juice and Worcestershire sauce, and stir over low heat for 5 minutes. Add the crab mixture to the cornmeal and mix carefully. Allow the stuffing to stand before proceeding.

Stuff the fish with this mixture. Close the cavity with small skewers and string. Place the closed fish on its side on a rack in a baking pan. Brush the top side of the fish with butter, and bake in a preheated 400°F oven for 10 minutes for each inch thickness of the stuffed fish, approximately 25-35 minutes, depending on the size of the fish. Pour the sherry and water beneath the fish and baste. Cover with foil to avoid scorching if necessary.

This makes 3 cups of stuffing, enough for four "school" trout, but more than necessary for a single two-pound fish unless you remove the backbone.

WHY WE GO DOWN TO THE WATER

I'm holding an old bamboo fly rod that has seen better days. Its color is a faded maroon and the varnish is gone in most places, rubbed through by three generations of trout fishermen. Stamped on the reel seat it reads "F.E. Thomas, Special, Bangor, ME." When I put the three sections together, there is a definite cast off in the tip, testament to the hours my great grandfather spent on summer evenings during the 1920s, trolling Woods Lake high in the Colorado mountains.

With his rod lodged in the fantail of his small rowboat, Robert Culberson plowed the water. He liked to say he was "rowing for fish" with a bright streamer trailing in his wake. But there was more than fishing at issue.

A single pull on the oars would send his boat into a long glide, oars lifted and dripping briefly, serenely entering the world of the mountains at twilight. In the shadows of a pine, a porcupine might emerge to tempt a morsel, or a deer and her fawn drop their heads for an instant at water's edge to steal a drink.

Occasionally a rainbow trout would rise to the lure tied behind Culberson's rod. A two foot long fish, no longer happy with a diet of insects, would take the imitation minnow and be drawn swiftly onboard for the short row home.

Culberson's family looked on from afar. Drawn up in wicker chairs beside the cottage, they watched the shadows creep across the lawn that ran down to the water. This was the family's summer pilgrimage to the high, cool mountains. A fishing place, a wilderness place, with a smokehouse stoked with willow sticks that brought that rainbow full circle in the cycle of catching and eating in a restrained and decorous way.

This was a modern man, lifted briefly from the temple of the city, and paddling as hard as he could to share again in the primitive world quickly fading beyond his grasp. Why would anyone in this century row around a lake at twilight? It had something to do with the fish, but also the weather, and the deer and the porcupines.

Thousands of us make this pilgrimage every year. Fabled waters and distant locations beckon with a challenge, and those of us steeped in a great respect for the lore of rivers and of fishing, are grateful for a chance to participate. Perhaps we need to feel the same currents that washed about the boots of Skues or Halford or John Tainter Foote. Perhaps we need to fish the shadows and to feel the chill of history and tradition.

"... I have fished the Beaverkill, and have seen the rise at ... Barnhart's Pool reminiscent of the old days on the river ... I know that I cannot escape this feeling [of respect] ... when the twilight falls and I am alone with the river. One almost expects to round a bend and find the ghost of Richard Robbins, and to be hailed by the old man to tie on a fly for him in the failing light of age and evening." (*Matching the Hatch*, Earnest G. Schwiebert, Jr., Macmillan Company, 1955)

And we all hope for such an encounter. The sound of the stream, the shadow of a fish or the darting minnows among the stones, each in their way remind us of past seasons and other fishers who have worked this same river. With all temporal baggage left behind at the water's edge, the trout fisherman is free to contemplate the beauty of small things, and to bend his worldly achievements to a primitive's respect for nature.

I went once to a chalk stream in England for that very reason. I was honored to be invited for a day on the Test River, the stuff of dreams. This is where it all began.

There would be no dry-fly fishing today but for this river's slow moving, insect rich, chalkstone filtered waters. Frederick Halford was tutored there. Theodore Gordon took up those techniques and spread them in a mantle across America that covers every river, fast or small, in the trout fishing world.

But the Test is not any river. It is contemplative. Romsey Abbey, which is nestled against its meandering banks, encouraged its monks in ancient times to fish for trout because such conduct "was seemly, and did not disturb their duty of continual contemplation of divine matters."

One look at the Test and I was fascinated. At first you notice the lushness of the pastures and the subtle, understated banks of the stream. Then you are drawn to the transparent, utter clarity of the water. It is reminiscent of the Letort Spring Creek in Pennsylvania, but with a haircut. The submerged grasses are manicured and combed to maintain the correct balance between water and cover. The walkways are marked and brushed. There are river wardens whose lives are dedicated to a single stretch of the river, and they take their work very seriously. Good fish are protected, and predatory fish are "removed." It is an entirely predictable river. We expect that of the English.

But they barely know what to expect of us.

I was decked out with every known item of gear: moleskin plus fours, glare free polaroid glasses, and hemostats jabbed into my lapel in the event a ferocious fish had to be wrestled down and unhooked. I also had my wife and a guest dog, a young cocker Spaniel named Teddy, sent along as observer of this epochal conflict between man and river, and promised by his owner to be very well behaved.

Our minder for this expedition, hardly a guide or a gillie but more like a museum docent, showed us the drawn beat on the river. I was reminded of being shown around someone's garden to admire the azaeleas in bloom. All was in perfect order. Without effort one could see straight through the tranquil current, identifying every rock, bug or grass at the bottom of the stream which was nowhere more than 6 or 8 feet deep, and narrow enough to throw a brick across in most places. It was a fairy tale and I felt that I had arrived at the Holy See. While it lasted.

Just past the "rain shed," a "pet" brown trout was feeding happily on spent flies floating past. I don't recall that this particular fish actually had a Christian name, but everything else about him was well known. At the second

rise I began to offer a Grey Wulff, recommended for fishing the Test by Lord Home in a book called *Reflections on Field and Stream.*

My technique was cramped and after several casts, I still had not gotten the range or the float I wanted. The minder was addressing me in subdued tones, offering suggestions on my back cast when his voice froze in a strangled gasp of air.

I turned in time to see Teddy, the cocker, leaping over the grassy bank, his ears outstretched to either side like helicopter rotors as he soared and crashed onto his prey, the unsuspecting trout. It was all very humiliating, rather like having your child fling a frisbee over the bowed heads at the Easter cathedral service.

The dog was retrieved, and marched to the car. The trout was unhurt, and after a reasonable amount of bowing and scraping I was asked to return to fishing, "perhaps a bit upstream," where I met with a modest success. The caught fish was quickly released by our minder, with one eye over his shoulder in the direction of the car.

That was the end of my duel with the river. Having caught trout on the Test, I can now look any trout fisherman in the eye. I have been to the mountain, so to speak. I have cast flies in the fabled water. I know firsthand the beauty and the style of that river. I can tell the tale, but I rarely mention the dog.

There is a parallel here to the many accomplished fishermen whose respect for the river and its fishes compels them to catch-and-release as a matter of course. They demonstrate consummate skill with high parabolic arcs on the back cast, and thoughtful rolls under overhanging trees on the delivery. They recognize the emerging Hex and Mayfly patterns, and they are meticulous in the selection of their tied offerings. Yet, they abstain from killing and eating.

It is a demonstration of their respect for the life in the water and the ethos of trout fishermen that entitles them to a good and righteous swagger. Their abstention would have seemed quite bizarre to the ancient monks of Romsey. But it is their passion.

For contrast, spare a moment for the drama of fishing Alaska. Picture the swagger photo in which she is holding a Rainbow that was twelve pounds when it came to the net. Her pigtails are tumbling out of her otherwise all-business Judith Bowman cap with its distinctive logo of the "uncaged woman." You hardly notice the large caliber revolver she carries for bears, or the fly mask for protection against mosquitoes the size of sparrows. Everything

in her earnest smile says: she played it by the rules, all the way. That is respect for the river.

And since that day I watched Peter O'Reilly dapping for trout on Ireland's Lake Sheelin, my view of lake fishing has never been the same. As we set out, there was a bright chop on the water. Three miles out the wild swans that called Midras Cove home rose up with a gaggle and circled us in the sky, berating our intrusion.

With a large streamer at the end of his line, O'Reilly also fished two drop lines. In rhythm to the pitching of the small boat he dapped the two drop flies and caused them to dance across the water's surface, creating a splatter pattern for the fish below. Trout will rise to this intrusion, and they did. That night we ate fresh brown trout poached in milk and sorrel from the garden on the day they were caught.

The love of that big water, and the practical grasp of the many techniques of presenting these artful flies to deep trout, all the while with a hand on the oar of a brightly painted boat, speaks of the love and respect of that man which is echoed in his many books on Irish trout.

On many a winter's night, fishermen have shown their respect for the rivers by taking solace from the insights of Izaak Walton, who even though he wasn't a dry-fly fisherman, was a devoted pastoral gentleman, who found his destiny in fishing. His books were written out of a love and knowledge of the sport, and the thrill of participating in another world.

Another such searcher was named Roderick Haig-Brown. He spent a lifetime in British Columbia, fishing and writing about the Columbia River, its fish and, incidentally, its people. His chronicles of the life cycles of the river will be read for centuries more.

"... I remember the approach to the Sandy Pool — under the white-barked alders a floor of fresh-swept sand pierced by bleeding heart and a thousand trilliums and the pink Easter lilies just breaking out of bud. Once, going up to the Canyon Pool along the far bank of the river, I crossed a little swamp where skunk cabbage flowers sprang stongly from black ooze in spaced and loveliest yellow. There is pink almond blossom in April, and heavy white cherry blossom against blue and white skies. There are killdeer and yellowlegs on the tide flats, meadow larks on the fence posts, red-winged blackbirds in the swamps. Not to go out and meet all this would be a denial of the year's hope." (*A River Never Sleeps*, Roderick Haig-Brown, p. 86-87)

Each of these lovers of the trout had their own special river. A.J. McClane loved to talk about the "fishing hut" he shared with Vince Marinaro on the Letort River in Pennsylvania's Cumberland Valley. That network of great trout waters included Watercress Bog, and the nearby Yellow Breeches, Boiling Springs, and other small creeks running over limestone that created river conditions quite similar to the English chalkstone rivers.

It was there that Marinaro created the "jassid" or leaf hopper imitation tied sparsely with only silk thread, two wound hackels, short fibered and flattened by one jungle cock nail. This was an original American, a tiny golden backed bug that Joe Brooks described as a "pepper speck on the tongue." Incidentally, Brooks took Marinaro's "jassid" back to the Hampshire downs and caught trout on the Itchen River with it.

Show me a trout fisherman with a cherished, well-cared-for rod, a creel and a small metal box of insect imitations prepared with excruciating attention to detail and I will show you a true respecter of the river and of nature, and not merely a predator on the make.

Years ago I was in a village near Swansea, Wales. One fine old gentleman in a tweed jacket and ratcatcher cap was wading the flow, fishing beyond the arched stone bridge that separates the town from the rugby pitch. He was a retired schoolmaster, a friend and teacher to the lads at Mumbles Rugby Club, and he fished this spot of the river in his thoughtful, unhurried way.

For him, the walk down through the village and along the shingle to his river was the joy of the week. If he brought up a single fish, that was the end of the wading. He would walk proudly home, back up the cobbled village streets, with fish in hand, smiling and nodding gently to his neighbors on the way home to his kitchen.

I knocked on his cottage door and asked about the fishing. He showed me the frugal and practical equipment he used. The leaders, tied up during the winter, carried him through a dignified and productive spring. Once a week, if he was lucky, a trout was breaded and oven baked, with a helping of laver bread from the sea on his plate.

He used a four piece rod made from old Tonkin cane that had come down through his family, rather like the F.E. Thomas that I'm holding. According to my pal Marty Keane, Fred Thomas was known to use this mahogany finish on his favorite rods, and following the fashion of Leonard factory protégés, the rod is festooned with decorative intermediate wraps every inch or so along the rod.

I will probably never fish this old Thomas rod again. It shouldn't go on the salt water, and anyway, it's a little brittle, not to mention the "cast off." But I know when I run it through my hands that it has spent its days on the water, and it has worked against the currents and the weathers and it has fished with some dignity and a little success. For all of that, it has my respect and I can only hope for as much from those who hold it after me.

SPOTTED SEATROUT IN ASPIC

Buffet par excellence! The seatrout is as big as a salmon, as delicately flavored as a mountain trout, and benefits from lightly flavored aspics and garnishes. By removing the skin after cooking, the fish's shape is preserved, and the serving is more straight forward.

1 spotted seatrout, dressed (or spotted weakfish or lake trout)
16 cups Court Bouillon *(see page 73)*
8 cups of Aspic for Trout *(see page 74)*
2 large scallions, with tops
1 large radish

1 egg white, cooked and sliced into floral patterns
1 stuffed olive
6 Tomatoes Piquante *(see page 77)*
6 Stuffed Mushrooms *(see page 76)*
3 lemons, quartered and swathed in cheese cloth, as garnish
large fish poacher

The trout must first be scaled, washed and dried. Prepare the trout for poaching by trussing the cavity closed with kitchen twine. Circle around the fish from the head to tail and back, and tie. Place the fish in a poacher, and add cold court bouillon to cover. If the fish is too large for the poacher the head may be severed, cooked separately and rejoined on the serving platter. *(See page 84 for an illustrated description for preparing sea trout.)*

Bring the court bouillon to a low boil, and then reduce to a steady simmer until cooked. The fish is cooked after simmering for 10 minutes per inch of thickness of fish measured behind the gills, or when the dorsal fin flakes easily to the point of a knife.

Using the poaching basket, remove the fish from the court bouillon and allow it to drain and cool.

Lay the fish on a smooth work surface on its side, and remove the kitchen twine. Remove the skin from the top side, together with any discoloration, fins, or loose bits.

Decorate the fish on a serving platter using thin strips of scallions, radish, and cooked egg white, arranged in a floral pattern and bathed in aspic as demonstrated on page 85. Replace the fish's eye with a stuffed olive

Garnish the platter with decorative Tomatoes Piquante and Stuffed Mushrooms following the directions on pages 76-77. Serve cold with lemon mayonnaise and lemon wedges wrapped in cheesecloth.

RED TROUT — GREEN SAUCE

High country watercress brings a bright contrast to the red meated steelheads and other trout who feed on crustaceans. The steelhead has been reclassified more than once, but in the kitchen we are not slaves to taxonomy, and still serve this green sauce that A.J. McClane so loved.

1 steelhead filet, (1½ pounds, boned, skin on)
1 Tablespoon lemon juice and water for poaching
1 cup scallions, chopped
1 clove garlic, chopped
3 Tablespoons Crayfish Butter *(see page 75)*
2 cups fish fumet or stock *(see page 73)*

1 cup potatoes, skinned and sliced thinly
3 cups fresh watercress, chopped
salt and pepper
4 Tablespoons heavy cream
1 cup crayfish tails, cooked

In a large sauté pan, soften the scallions and garlic in the 3 tablespoons of crayfish butter for 3-5 minutes. Add the potatoes and the fish stock, reduce to a simmer, and cook for 30 minutes, uncovered, allowing the mixture to reduce somewhat to 1 generous cup.

In a pan large enough to accommodate the filet without bending, add water to cover and the lemon juice. Introduce the filet and bring the water to a simmer and continue for about 10-12 minutes until the fish is done. The flesh will be firm to the touch and flake to the point of a knife. Remove and drain the filet and keep warm.

To prepare the green sauce:

Add the watercress to the reduced potato/stock mixture in the sauté pan and heat through over moderate heat for 3-5 minutes. Purée this mixture in a food processor, in batches if necessary, and return to the sauté pan. Over low heat, gradually add the cream. Adjust the seasonings with salt and white pepper and add the cooked crayfish tails.

Serve the filet with the green sauce over and fresh watercress to garnish.

Sauté of Trout Amandine

This is one of the Big Three among the canon of familiar trout dishes. The blanched and slivered almonds
rolled in butter and electrified with a dash of lemon juice bring a contrast of textures to the dish that has become a culinary staple.

2 small brook trout — heads, tails, and fins removed
¼ cup flour
1 teaspoon salt
freshly ground black pepper
2 Tablespoons butter
1 Tablespoon olive oil

2 Tablespoons sherry, sweet or cream style
3 Tablespoons butter
1 cup almonds, slivered and blanched
2 Tablespoons lemon juice
lemon wedges for garnish

Combine the flour, salt and pepper on a large cutting board, and daub the trout in the flour until thoroughly coated on both sides.

Warm the butter and olive oil in a skillet over moderate heat and sauté the trout spread eagle, flesh side down for five minutes, then flesh side up for five minutes. After turning the fish, sprinkle 1 tablespoon of sherry over each fish and continue the sauté until cooked. The trout are done when the flesh is firm to the touch, with a golden color. Remove the trout as they are done to a warm platter and reserve. Remove any burned bits from the pan.

Melt the remaining 3 tablespoons of butter over low heat and cook the almonds, stirring to prevent burning for 3 minutes. Remove the skillet from the heat, add the lemon juice and scrape with a spatula to mix the contents before spooning over the individual trout, and garnish with the lemon wedges.

CRACKER FRIED TROUTLINGS

One of the miracles of the modern hatchery trout is that in three or four months you have a delectable
dart-sized rainbow "sardine" that can be swirled in cracker crumbs, quick fried, and passed around as finger food.

4 cups troutlings — dressed, 4 inches long each
4 cups saltine crackers, whole
2 eggs, slightly beaten
2 Tablespoons ice water
2 teaspoons salt

2 teaspoons fresh cracked pepper
2 teaspoons ground cayenne pepper
1 teaspoon ground comino
vegetable oil for frying

These small fish can be cooked quickly in hot oil. The cooking heat renders the few remaining bones edible.

In a processor, reduce the crackers to very fine crumbs. Add the salt, pepper, cayenne and comino and blend thoroughly. Pour the cracker mixture in a paper bag.

Roll each fish in the beaten egg, then drop a few at a time into the paper bag. Shake the bag to coat the troutlings, then remove each fish separately and shake to remove excess cracker meal.

Preheat the oil to 375°F in a large heavy pan. Fry the fish a handful at a time and remove quickly with a strainer or slotted spoon as they brown. Keep the cooked fish warm in a 200°F oven until ready to serve.

Serve with horseradish sauce.

Chinese Basket Trout, Steamed with Ginger/Scallion Sauce

*Steam is the purest cooking medium, and produces the most moist fish. In these durable
willow chambers, the fish quickly develops a spontaneous sauce or essence that flavors the small bits of rice and ginger.*

4 small brook trout, 10-11 inches each, cleaned and boned
6 scallions, split on the long axis
2 Tablespoons fresh ginger, skinned and finely diced
2 teaspoons brown sugar
2 Tablespoons soy sauce
1 Tablespoon sesame oil (or olive oil)
2 Tablespoons dry sherry

1 teaspoon lemon juice
¼ teaspoon tobasco sauce
1 cup rice, cooked
water for steaming and rice
a wok and two chinese steamer baskets with one lid
2 soup bowls fitted to the baskets

Place 2-3 inches of water in a wok or large Dutch oven and, over high heat, bring the water to a boil.

Select two shallow soup bowls sufficiently small enough so that each will fit inside one of the steamer baskets leaving a slight space around the edges for the steam to rise. The bowls will eventually hold ½ cup sauce in addition to the fish and rice.

Place ½ cup rice in the bottom of each soup bowl. Lightly salt and pepper all the trout, inside and out, then place 2 scallion strips and a pinch of fresh ginger inside each fish. Fold the sides over to hold the seasonings. Place two fish in each bowl, head to tail across the rice, and cover each fish with 1 additional scallion strip and an equal portion of the remaining ginger.

In a small bowl combine the brown sugar, soy sauce, oil, sherry, lemon juice, and tobasco sauce and stir until the sugar is dissolved. Sprinkle 1 tablespoon of this sauce over each fish. Stack the soup bowls in the steamer baskets, and stack the steamer baskets on top of one another. Cover and place over the wok, or on a rack in a Dutch oven. More than two steamer baskets at a time reduces the heat in the top basket.

The fish is done after steaming 10 minutes for each inch of fish thickness, plus 2 minutes for each steamer in the stack. Test for doneness on the upper level. Carefully decant the bowls, being careful to preserve the liquid in each bowl, and serve immediately.

SMOKING RAINBOWS

*In a quieter time fishermen gathered up aspen and willow to flavor the cool wood smoke that brought their rainbows
to a shimmering perfection. Smoked trout eaten the next day is at its best and allows us a window back into our primitive past.*

6 rainbow trout — whole, cleaned with no gills
1 quart fresh water
¼ cup salt
½ cup honey

1 teaspoon white pepper, freshly cracked
½ cup lemon juice
3 teaspoons fresh dill, chopped
additional water to cover

In the morning of the day you intend to smoke the fish, prepare the brine as follows. Simmer the salt, honey, pepper, lemon juice and dill in the quart of water until the salt and honey are dissolved.

Pour the mixture into a masonry crock or very large pickle jar tall enough for the fish to stand on end.

Introduce the fish into the brine and soak six hours for 10-12 inch trout. In warm weather the crock should be moved into the refrigerator and covered. Stir occasionally.

Remove the fish and rinse briefly in cold water. Arrange the fish on a rack and allow them to dry in the air for an hour or so. A glaze, called a pellicle, will form over the fish which indicates they are ready for smoking.

Using an electric smoker, allow a dense smoke to build up with aromatic wood shavings. Hang the fish by cotton string around the tail or using small "s" shaped hooks inserted through the mandible of each fish. Spread open the body cavity of each fish with two toothpicks, one at the head, the other near the tail, and hang the fish as far apart as possible inside the smoker to assure maximum circulation.

Two cups of wood shavings burned up through the process is enough smoke flavor. Allow the drying to continue for a total of three hours at 110°F, and test for dryness with a fork. The fish is done when it flakes easily at the thickest point. Serve immediately or store in airtight containers. Moisture is the enemy of smoked foods and their quality goes off over time. There is nothing wrong with eating freshly smoked fish; in fact, it is the best.

Irish Poached Trout in Sorrel Court Bouillon

Fresh sorrel from country gardens brings a slightly acidic balance to the poaching liquid. Use as much sorrel as you can find, the larger leaves are more bitter than the small, and supplement the court bouillon with cross sections of lemon, seeds removed.

2 trout — whole, dressed, gills removed
2 cups milk
1 lemon
12 cups water
2 Tablespoons sea salt

2 cups sorrel leaves, chopped (2 Tablespoons reserved for the trout)
2 whole sorrel leaves
salt and pepper
fish poacher
kitchen cotton string

In a large saucepan combine half the water, salt and the chopped sorrel leaves, reserving 2 Tablespoons of the chopped sorrel leaves for the inside of the two fish. Bring the mixture to a simmer, stirring to dissolve all the salt, and allowing the chopped sorrel to wilt for 10 minutes without boiling. Remove from the heat and allow to cool. Add the reserved 6 cups of water.

Peel the lemon, remove the pith, and slice in thin round sections. Remove the seeds. Place the lemon sections in the bottom of the fish poacher, add the milk, and the cooled or tepid sorrel water.

Lightly salt and pepper the inside of each trout. Sprinkle 1 Tablespoon of the reserved chopped sorrel inside each fish. Fold 1 long sorrel leaf in half on the long axis and lay inside each trout.

Close the trout, and double wrap the cavity closed snugly with string tied in a knot under the chin. Repeat for the second fish, and place both fish in the cool or tepid Sorrel Court Bouillon. Add water if necessary to reach level with the fish.

Place the poacher on the fire and bring quickly to a simmer, and cover. Allow the fish to cook at a bare simmer, but never a boil, for 10 minutes for each inch of thickness, or until done. Remove the fish from the pan, drain, and slide carefully onto a warmed plate. Remove the string.

Serve with Diplomate Sauce *(see page 76)* or Lemon Mayonnnaise *(see page 77)*.

Welsh Sea Trout with Seaweed Laver Bread

Sturdy trout filets browned in bread crumbs and oven baked on a sheet are traditional Welsh fish. The sumptuous green seaweed cakes called laver, with just a hint of oysters and the ocean in them, were the Celtic "found food" of ancient time. Nowadays, the laver bread is teased out of translucent sheets of seaweed from the Oriental market.

4 sea trout filets, skinned and washed
3 Tablespoons lemon juice
salt and pepper
4 teaspoons olive oil
6 eggs, beaten
4 cups stale bread crumbs, no crusts, finely crumbled

parsley for garnish
For Seaweed Laver Bread:
  2 envelopes of laver (14 sheets dried seaweed)
  1 cup warm water
  1½ cup rolled oats.
  4 Tablespoons olive oil

Clean the filets, then cut into rectangles about 3 by 5 inches by ¾ inch thick. Rub both sides with the lemon juice, then season with salt and pepper. Dip each filet in the beaten eggs, then in the fine bread crumbs, and place on a shallow, greased roasting pan.

Bake the filets in a preheated oven at 400° F for 10 minutes. Turn the fish, and continue baking for an additonal 10 minutes, or until the crust is brown.

Serve on warm plates with parsley, a splash of Worcestershire Sauce, and a serving of Seaweed Laver Bread patties.

Seaweed Laver Bread:

Laver is easily obtainable from Oriental markets. The seaweed variety *Porphyra tenera* is called *nori* in Japan and is practically identical to the kind once gathered up along the beaches in Wales at low tide.

In a large open dish, soften the dried sheets of laver in the water for 30 minutes. Drain and discard the excess water. In a processor bowl, combine the laver and the oats, and process for 10 seconds. Scrape down the sides of the bowl, and process for another 10 seconds.

Form the laver bread into patties about three inches wide and ¾ inch thick. This recipe should make 8 patties. Refrigerate 30 minutes or longer, until needed.

In olive oil over medium high heat, sauté the laver bread patties for about 5 minutes a side, not allowing the oates to burn. Remove and serve immediately.

Truite au Bleu

Blue trout never photograph well. Just the rush to get the fish cleaned and into the pot in ten minutes is a challenge. Nevertheless, it is the "ne plus ultra" of pure troutness. Serve on a linen napkin with Lemon Mayonnaise, and treat yourself to what trout is all about.

8 trout caught within the hour
2 quarts Court Bouillon de Vinaigre *(See recipe for Court Bouillon with Wine on page 73; substitute red vinegar for the wine.)*

8 teaspoons vinegar
2 cups potato balls, boiled
1 cup parsley, chopped
lemon wedges for garnish

Prepare the court bouillon ahead of time and allow it to simmer 30 minutes. Bring it to a boil again at the time of killing the fish.

Do not handle the skin of these fish more than necessary, for it is in the preserving of the natural coating over the skin that the blue color emerges. Quickly kill the fish with a blow to the skull a la trout priest and clean them through the gills. Remove all viscera and gills, leaving the belly intact. Alternatively, you may dress them in the familiar manner, but they should not be handled much or scaled, frozen or put back in water after dressing.

Rub the skin of each fish with a teaspoon of the vinegar, and then plunge them into the boiling vinegar court bouillon. In eight minutes, the vinegar, skin film and natural proteins of the fish will turn the skin blue, and the fish will curl slightly, head to tail. The skin of the fish may burst in places and this is considered a confirmation of freshness. This is the essence of fresh trout. They should be removed, drained and served immediately on a bold linen napkin, with the boiled potatoes and parsley, and a lemon to hand.

Sauté of Small Trout with Basil Sauce

Delicate fish, completely boned, absorb the cooking flavors into the meat more successfully.
The cooking liquid is then combined with the basil, oil and garlic to finish with a very bright sauce.

2 brook trout — boned filets, head and tail off
2 Tablespoons olive oil
2 scallions, thinly sliced with tops
1 garlic clove, sliced
2 Tablespoons fresh rib of celery, thinly sliced
2 cups white wine

½ teaspoon dried thyme
salt and pepper
2 garlic cloves, peeled and sliced before processing
2 cups fresh basil leaves, tightly packed
2 Tablespoons virgin olive oil
salt and pepper

Heat 2 tablespoons of olive oil in a large sauté pan and soften the scallions, garlic and celery slices over moderate heat for up to 10 minutes. Do not allow the vegetables to color. Add 1 cup of wine, increase the heat, and reduce the wine to a syrupy essence. Avoid scorching. Add the second cup of wine, the thyme, salt and pepper and allow the sauce to simmer for an additional 3 minutes over low heat.

Remove the pan from the heat, and when the sauce is cool to the touch, add the filets, skin side down. Bring the sauce to a simmer over a hot burner. Allow the fish to simmer for only a total of 3 minutes. Do not turn, but baste with a spoon, then remove the pan from the heat. Filets thicker than ¾ inch may take longer, and are done when the flesh is firm and flakes to the tip of a knife.

Remove the filets to warmed serving plates and reserve. In a food processor, blend the garlic, basil leaves, salt, pepper, and 2 tablespoons olive oil and process for 3 seconds. Add ¼ cup or more of the sauté juices, and process until thoroughly combined. Serve this basil sauce over the filets with a Heart of Romaine salad.

TROUT MONTE CARLO STYLE

The Hotel Paris in Monaco knew the secret of small trout cookery. Sealed inside a jacket of blanched lettuce leaves,
the trout was flavored with a dash of sherry and fresh tarragon, and finished with a butter, wine and cream sauce.

4 trout, cleaned and boned with heads on, fins removed
1 teaspoon thyme, ground
2–3 large Boston lettuce heads, leaves separated
1 cup shallots, sliced thinly
1 or 2 cups white wine, to generously cover the bottom
   of the pan
3 teaspoons butter
salt and pepper
½ cup cream for the sauce

4 cups stuffing made with:
   2 Tablespoons butter
   1 Tablespoon olive oil
   2 Tablespoons brandy
   1 cup celery, diced
   1 cup onions, diced
   1 cup mushrooms, diced
   1 cup scallions and tops, chopped finely
   ½ teaspoon each of salt and pepper

In a large sauté pan, combine 2 tablespoons softened butter, 1 tablespoon olive oil and the brandy. Sauté the celery, onions, mushrooms and scallions over moderate heat for 3-5 minutes until thoroughly softened. Add salt and pepper and stir for another 3 minutes. Remove and cool.

Prepare 2–3 large lettuce leaves for each fish. Parboil the individual leaves in boiling water for 3–5 minutes, then remove, separate and allow to cool. Lightly salt and pepper each fish, inside and out. Spread a pinch of ground thyme around the inside of each cavity, then stuff the cavity with a share of the stuffing. Wrap the leaves in an overlapping pattern around each fish, first down its belly, then down its back, using 2–3 leaves at least for each fish.

Butter an open roasting dish large enough for the fish, and sprinkle the shallots on the bottom. Lay the fish side by side with space between them. Salt and pepper, and add sufficient wine to cover the bottom of the dish. Put the remaining ½ teaspoon butter equally on top of each fish.

Place the trout in an oven pre-heated to 400°F, immediately reducing the temperature to 375°F. Bake the trout for 10 minutes per inch of thickness, basting. Transfer the wrapped fish to a serving dish, and keep warm.

Pour the liquid left in the baking dish into a saucepan and, over high heat for 3–5 minutes, reduce to a syrupy essence. Add the cream, and bring to a light boil. Remove from the heat and whisk in the butter. Serve the fish on individual plates with the sauce poured over.

Braised Trout a la Chambord

*Chambord Palace was over the top in every category. The stables housed 1,200 horses, the great hall had armor
and weapons for a hundred men, and the kitchen was the size of a hockey rink. And they put everything they had into their trout, too!*

4 trout — ½ pound each, whole, cleaned and gilled
2 cups shrimp, raw and shelled
2 egg whites
⅓ cup cream
½ teaspoon salt
½ teaspoon fresh cracked white pepper
½ teaspoon nutmeg

¼ cup breadcrumbs
½ teaspoon cayenne pepper
I teaspoon bouquet garni
I½ cups white wine
I Tablespoon butter
I cup mushrooms, thinly sliced
2 cups cooked white rice

Refrigerate the bowl and blade of the food processor and all ingredients for the stuffing. Beat the egg whites with a whisk to form soft peaks. In a processor bowl, combine the shrimp, egg whites, cream, salt, pepper, nutmeg, and cayenne pepper. Process until the mixture is thoroughly incorporated. Add the breadcrumbs and pulse twice more.

Stuff the trout with an equal share of the mixture, and place all trout together in a well buttered baking dish. Add ½ cup wine and the bouquet garni and bake in a pre-heated oven at 375° F for up to 15 minutes because of the stuffing, basting often.

Remove the fish to a platter and keep warm. Remove the sauce to a saucepan. Add the mushrooms and the final glass of wine and simmer for 5 minutes, reducing slightly. Serve the fish over a bed of rice with the sauce poured over each fish, garnished with parsley.

SUPPORTING RECIPES

Court Bouillon with Wine

1 large leek, sliced thinly
1 celery rib, sliced
1 carrot, sliced
2 cups of onions, sliced
1 cup parsley sprigs
1 bay leaf

½ teaspoon dried thyme
salt
6 cups water
2 cups wine, red or white
5 black peppercorns

In a large Dutch oven combine the vegetables, water and a small pinch of salt and bring to a boil. Reduce the heat and simmer for 15 minutes. Add the wine and simmer for 15 additional minutes. At 12 minutes, add the peppercorns and do not allow the mixture to boil. Allow to cool slightly, then strain before using.

Fish Fumet

2 pounds of fish heads, bones, skin and trimmings
1 celery rib, sliced
1 carrot, sliced
1 onion, sliced

1 Tablespoon of bouquet garni in a bag or infuser
salt and pepper
12 cups water
2 cups white wine, dry

In a large saucepan combine the fish, vegetables and water. Bring to a boil and simmer over low heat for 15 minutes, skimming off the scum that rises to the top. Season lightly with salt and pepper and, over low heat, simmer for 10 minutes further, covered. Add the wine and simmer for 10 additional minutes, covered.

Remove, cool, and strain without pressing, and reserve the fumet for aspic or further reduction. *(See page 88 for illustrated instructions for making fish fumet.)*

Aspic for Trout

6 cups of fish fumet
3 egg whites
3 packages of powdered gelatin
1 teaspoon green peppercorns, crushed

½ teasoon dried thyme
1 Tablespoon lemon juice
salt
⅓ cup Madeira (or dry sherry)

In 1 cool cup of the fish fumet, soften the 3 packages of gelatin and reserve. Combine the peppercorns, thyme and lemon juice with the remainder of the fish fumet in a 2-3 quart saucepan. Adjust the seasoning and add salt if necessary.

Stir in the softened gelatin and the beaten egg whites. Whisking constantly over high heat, bring the mixture to a boil. As the liquid begins to rise in the pot threatening to boil over, whisk twice more and remove the saucepan from the heat. Allow the saucepan to stand undisturbed for 5 minutes.

Place a large sieve over a deep bowl. Line the sieve with a cotton kitchen towel soaked in cold water and wrung dry. Slowly pour all of the contents of the saucepan, eggs and fumet into the sieve. Do not touch until all the translucent aspic has dripped through.

Remove the sieve, add ⅓ cup of Madeira to the aspic and cool. Place the deep bowl of aspic in a bed of ice to accelerate its setting, or in a sink of hot water to retard the rate, pending preparation of the trout.

DeZanger's Dutch Butter Sauce

8 Tablespoons butter
1 cup sour cream
4 egg yolks, well beaten
1 Tablespoon prepared mustard

1 Tablespoon parsley, chopped
salt and pepper
1 Tablespoon lemon juice
2 Tablespoons lemon rind, finely chopped

In a saucepan over low heat, or in a double boiler, soften the butter then add small amounts of the cream and alternately the beaten egg yolks, whisking all the while, until the mixture begins to thicken. Add the mustard, parsley, salt and pepper to taste while whisking continuously. Add the lemon juice and rind. Whisk twice and allow to heat through. Whisk again before serving. This is sufficient for 4 timbales.

Crayfish Butter

3 pounds of whole live crayfish
2 sticks butter (½ pound)
¼ teaspoon paprika

¼ teaspoon cayenne pepper
¼ cup clam juice (alternate: fish stock or hot water)

Purge the crayfish by placing them still alive in a kitchen sink or large bowl of water to cover with 1 Tablespoon of dissolved salt. Allow the crayfish to swim about, then select only live crayfish and drop them in a Dutch oven with 2 quarts of boiling water. Allow the water to return to a boil and continue cooking for 2-3 minutes. Remove from the heat and drain.

Peel the tail meat from the crayfish and set aside for another purpose, such as Diplomate Sauce *(see page 76)*. Reserve the shells, bodies, heads, claws, feet and debris of the crayfish, and chop roughly.

Melt ½ pound butter in a saucepan. Place the crayfish shells and bits in a processor bowl. Cover with the melted butter and process for 30 seconds, stopping and scraping as necessary. Empty the creamed butter and crayfish paste into a saucepan. Add ¼ cup clam juice and reheat, gently stirring, without allowing the butter to boil. Repeat the blender process, and then strain the flavored butter into a small bowl and refrigerate, stirring occasionally until it sets. This makes about ½ cup of crayfish butter.

DIPLOMATE SAUCE

2 cups fish fumet
1 cup red wine
2 Tablespoon Port wine
1 teaspoon arrowroot
2 Tablespoons crayfish butter

½ cup scalded cream
salt and pepper
4 Tablespoons cooked, chopped crayfish tails
2 Tablespoons chopped parsley

In a large saucepan, combine the fumet and red wine and reduce to 1 cup total. Dissolve the arrowroot in the Port wine. Off the fire, add the crayfish butter to the reduction and whisk. Add the hot cream and the Port wine with arrowroot to the reduction and whisk, returning to a low fire to thicken. Off the fire, rectify the seasonings by adding salt and pepper. Add the cooked crayfish tails and the parsley. Stir and send to the table.

STUFFED MUSHROOMS

6 crimini mushrooms
2 Tablespoons butter
2 Tablespoons lemon juice
½ cup beef bouillon

6 Tablespoons Blue Shroppshire cheese, crumbled
  (or Roquefort)
salt and pepper
3 green olives, sliced transversely into 2 pieces

Wash the mushrooms. Remove the stems, and reserve. Carefully peel the mushrooom caps and simmer together in a saucepan, basting with the melted butter, lemon juice and beef bouillon for 3 minutes. Remove and drain. The mushrooms should still be white underneath, and not overcooked.

Sprinkle the cheese over the inside of each upturned mushroom cap. Place one slice of green olive with pimento in the center of each cheese filled mushroom. Grill under the broiler for 5 minutes, and allow to cool before serving.

Tomatoes Piquante

12 cherry tomatoes, large and ripe
1 cup of French salad dressing (oil and vinegar type only)
12 egg yolks, hard boiled (reserve the white for floral design on trout)
12 Tablespoons sour cream

6 anchovy filets, flat and drained
1 teaspoon cayenne pepper
½ teaspoon each of salt and pepper
3 cured black olives, sliced in slivers, or small truffle pieces

Cut the top off each tomato, and trim the base so it will sit flat. With a small spoon remove the seeds and core at the center of each tomato. Fill each tomato with the oil and vinegar salad dressing and allow them to marinate for one hour in the refrigerator.

In a mixing bowl, combine the hard boiled egg yolks, sour cream and anchovy filets using the back of a fork until thoroughly blended. Add salt and pepper to taste.

Remove the tomatoes from the refrigerator, drain the marinade, and fill each tomato with the egg and sour cream mixture. Top each mixture with an olive slice or truffle tip, and garnish the platter of trout in aspic.

Lemon Mayonnaise

1 egg
1 egg yoke
1 Tablespoon lemon juice
3 Tablespoons lemon pulp, seeds and fibers out

1 Tablespoon dijon style mustard
¾ cup olive oil (or rosemary flavored)
salt and pepper

Combine the egg, egg yolk, lemon juice, pulp, 1 tablespoon of dijon style mustard, and 1 tablespoon of the olive oil in a processor bowl. Blend for 10 seconds. Slowly add the remaining oil into the processor — blending through the liquid drip hole is ideal — until all the oil is incorporated. Adjust the salt and pepper, then cover and refrigerate until needed.

CHEDDAR SCONES

1½ cups flour
1 cup cheddar cheese, grated
1 Tablespoon baking soda
1 teaspoon cream of tartar

½ teaspoon salt
2 eggs
1 cup buttermilk

In a large mixing bowl, combine the flour, cheese, baking soda, cream of tartar, and salt. In a small bowl, combine the eggs and buttermilk and mix thoroughly.

Without beating or excessive stirring, carefully pour the buttermilk mixture into the flour and cheese, rolling the combination with a large spoon to mix the components evenly.

When a dough has formed, turn it onto a floured work surface. Pull off pieces of dough the size of a hen's egg, flatten each one slightly, and pierce it with the tines of a fork. Place all the scones on a floured baking sheet and in an oven pre-heated to 400° F, bake for 10-15 minutes until the scones are firm, but not scorched.

Scottish Rant Bread

2¼ cups warm water
2 packets dry yeast
¼ cup molasses
1½ Tablespoons salt
½ cup melted vegetable shortening
2-3 cups bread flour
1 cup stoneground whole wheat flour

1 cup bran flakes, unsweetened
½ cup soy flour
1½ cups whole grain cereal
½ cup unsweetened wheat germ
A two piece bread cooking cloche, consisting of a dish
    and bell shaped lid made of pourous earthenware.

Sprinkle the yeast over ½ cup warm water in a small bowl. Stir until dissolved and let stand in a warm, draft free place to proof for about 5 minutes until the yeast foams.

In a large mixing bowl, combine 2 cups of bread flour, all of the additional flours, the bran flakes, the wheat germ, the cereal and the salt. Make a hollow in the center and pour in the yeast, molasses, shortening and remaining warm water. Combine with a wooden spoon, then incorporate the remaining cup of bread flour using both hands.

When the dough cleans the sides of the bowl, turn it out onto a floured work surface and knead for 5 minutes until the dough is elastic. Place the dough in an oiled bowl, cover with oiled plastic wrap and let the dough rise for 1 hour in a warm, draft free place.

Gently deflate the dough, and turn it out onto a floured surface and form it into a large round, about two-thirds the size of the baking dish. Sprinkle the baking dish with cornmeal and place the dough in the dish. Cover with oiled plastic wrap and allow the dough to rise again for an hour.

Soak the domed lid of the cloche in water for 30 minutes and preheat the oven to 400° F. Slash the top of the loaf diagonally 4 or 5 times with a serrated knife, shake off the excess water from the cloche lid and place the lid over the dough. Bake for 30 minutes. Remove the lid and continue baking at 375° F for an additional 20 minutes until the loaf is a deep golden brown and sounds hollow to a thump of the knuckles.

Allow the loaf to cool before serving.

CULINARY PROCEDURES ILLUSTRATED

PAPILLOTES FOR TROUT

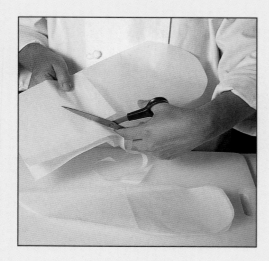

1.

Using brown culinary parchment, silicon covered only, cut a large rectangle, approximately 16 by 14 inches. Fold the parchment in half, and using the folded edge as the vertical line on one side, cut a large valentine in the shape of half a heart using kitchen scissors.

2.

Open the folded shape and place first the sauce and then the fish (or filet) in the center of each.

3.

Place a spoonful of the sauce in the cavity of the fish.

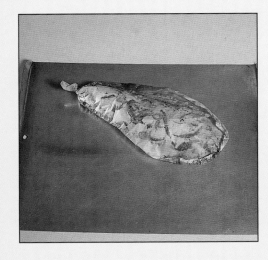

4.

Fold the papillote leaf over the fish and seal the edge. Begin by gripping a 2-inch length of double parchment at the top of the 'heart' and fold, and then fold again. Each fold need only be ¼ inch wide. Move 2 inches further along the seam and repeat, making sure that each successive fold overlaps its predecessor to close the envelope securely.

5.

Continue this folding until the entire lip is sealed and double twist the last section at the tip. Turn each papillote over so the folds are on the under side.

6.

Place the papillotes on an ungreased baking sheet and send to the oven immediately.

BUFFET OF SEA TROUT IN ASPIC

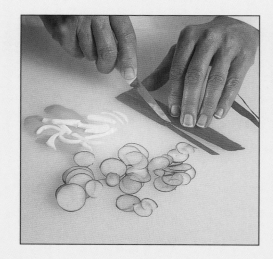

1.

Place a poached, cooled and refrigerated trout in the center of the serving platter. Using a spoon and a knife point, peel off the skin from one side of the fish, removing all bones, fins and discolored bits.

2.

Cut thin strips from the green part of the scallions, and recut into leaf shaped pieces. Cut thin discs from the cooked egg white, and subdivide these into flower petals. Cut thin rounds from the red skin of the radish.

3.

Dip each of the cut vegetables into the thickened and cooling aspic and arrange in a flower design on the exposed meat of the trout.

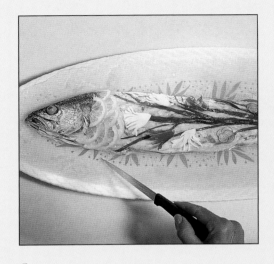

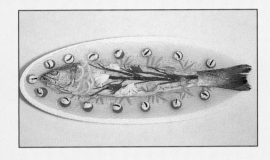

4.
Spoon the remaining aspic over the floral design, and over the entire trout. Coat the bottom and margins of the serving platter with the remaining aspic and allow to set in the refrigerator.

5.
After the aspic is set in the platter, use a dull knife blade to cut a criss-cross pattern of small cubes around the platter, forming aspic dice.

6.
Arrange the Tomatoes Piquante and Stuffed Mushrooms around the trout on the platter. Garnish with lemon halves wrapped in cheesecloth and serve with lemon mayonnaise.

TURBANS OF TROUT WITH CILANTRO MOUSSE

1.

Fold each refrigerated and seasoned filet into an oiled and refrigerated timbale with the white side of the fish to the outside, and press the fish lightly against the wall. Trim away any filet extending beyond the edges of the timbale and refrigerate again.

2.

Prepare the mousse by combining the parboiled, dried and cooled cilantro with the parsley, chives, basil leaf, and garlic purée, and process for 10 seconds.

3.

Beat the eggs, sherry, cayenne, salt and pepper, and turn this mixture into the processor with the cilantro. Combine for 10 seconds.

4.

In a chilled bowl whisk the egg whites until they hold slight peaks. Add this mixture to the processor bowl, and blend for 5 seconds.

In a bowl, beat the cream with a whisk until it holds slight peaks. Add this mixture to the processor bowl and blend for 5 seconds until thoroughly combined.

5.

Spoon the mousse into each timbale, and smooth flat at the top.

6.

Place the timbales in an open roasting pan. Add enough boiling water to reach ⅓ of the way up the timblale, but not enough to float them. Cover loosely with aluminum foil and bake for at least 60 minutes in a preheated oven at 350° F. The mousse is cooked when it becomes firm, and tends to draw away from the timbale. Remove from the oven, invert the timbales on a rack, and allow to cool. Refrigerate for at least one hour before decanting.

TURNING FUMET INTO DIPLOMATE SAUCE

1.

Assemble the best pieces of trimmings, skin and fish heads that are absolutely fresh. Fish scales left on the skin enhance the viscosity of the fumet, and can be strained away.

2.

Carefully slice the onion, leek, celery, and carrots. Place the bouquet garni in a muslin bag or tea infuser.

3.

Combine all the ingredients except the wine with water and simmer for 15 minutes skimming. Add the wine and continue skimming. This fumet can be used for aspic, or reduced to make fish sauces.

4.

To make Diplomate Sauce from the fumet, combine 2 cups of fish fumet with 1 cup of white wine and reduce over a hot fire to a total of 1 cup. Add 2 Tablespoons of Port wine in which has been dissolved 1 teaspoon of arrowroot.

5.

Remove from the fire and flavor with 2 Tablespoons of crayfish butter. Add ½ cup of scalded cream, stirring constantly, and rectify the seasonings by adding salt and pepper.

6.

Finish, off the fire, by adding 4 Tablespoons of cooked crayfish tails, chopped, and 2 Tablespoons of chopped parsley.

SUPPLIERS

Resa and Jon Wallach
Eden Brook Hatchery
1327 Cold Spring Road
Forestburgh, New York 12777
(914) 796-1749

Eden Brook Fish Market
73 Pleasant Street
Monticello, New York 12701
(914) 791-4345

Classic Rods & Tackle, Inc.
Martin J. Keane, Prop.
P.O.Box 288, Ashley Falls, Massachusetts 01222-0288
(413 229-7988

Trout Unlimited
1500 Wilson Boulevard, Suite 310
Arlington, VA 22209 - 2404
(703) 522-0200
To join or renew: 800-834-2419
http://www.tu.org.

Homarus, Inc.
76 Kisco Avenue,
Mt Kisco NY 10549
914-666-8992

Spence & Co. Limited
160 Manley St.
Brockton, MA 02401

INDEX